TWENTY MINUTES OF CALM

POEMS OF NATURE, SCENE & SEASON

DAVID MESSINEO

THE POET'S PRESS
Pittsburgh, PA

This is the 249th publication of
THE POET'S PRESS
2209 Murray Avenue #3
Pittsburgh, PA 15217-2338
www.poetspress.org

TABLE OF CONTENTS

To Kleber,
with love and gratitude for
28 years of calm
June 1991 to July 2019

When one gets quiet, then something wakes up inside one,
something quiet and happy like the stars.

— William Butler Yeats

In one of the stars I shall be living.
In one of them I shall be laughing.
And so it will be as if all the stars were laughing,
when you look at the sky at night ...
you, only you will have stars that can laugh!
But the eyes are blind.
One must look with the heart.

— Antoine de Saint-Exupery, *The Little Prince.*

PRELUDE

The Palace of Nine Perfections

On a painting in the Metropolitan Museum of Art,
New York City

A steep slant of *lapis lazuli* tile
leads the eye along this roof of
brilliant blue, curving to cornices
of carefully placed dragons.

From the bamboo railing,
I watch as the wind
pulls pine needles from the tree
perched precariously on the cliff.

While I stand in the soft safety of
this massive mountaintop palace,
I readily relate to
the fragility of the tree:

the merciless wind that picks
piece by piece, 'til branches are bare,
the solidity of soil
that lets needles renew.

And I revel quietly in
this rice paper moment:
the duality of something
so fragile, yet so strong.

<11>

TWENTY
MINUTES
OF CALM

Moment at Lake Atsion

In the New Jersey Pine Barrens, 2015

scrub pine curves
sideways question mark

cones burst, branch by branch
fanning over flickering ripples

words and pine cones interplay
mulling a Mullica meeting

pine needles notice the poet
painting time, pen to paper

tall logs face inward
framing the moment

beyond both, breeze brings
a Tibetan bell's chime

<15>

Eagle's Reach

The first thing you notice are the hands.
Each finger dark, each hand reaches from lands
and times millennia ago. They lance
in eerie white outlines of chalk,
the cave their sky. With animals, they dance
outlines into our times, and talk.

<16>

SATURDAY MORNING,
POUSADA MAR DE BÚZIOS

BÚZIOS, BRAZIL, 2005

Aquamarine Atlantic draws you in.
Pull back. Boats bob lazily,
musical notes dancing on
electric line staff. *Pull back*.
Five palm tree fronds flutter
in Búzios breeze, perhaps
paintbrush for the colored trims
decorating harbor boats.
Pan right. At Passeio de Bario,
men lean in as the stand begins
cooking fresh fish for this afternoon.
Pan left. Dolphin statue oversees
serene scene, poised passively on the
aqua blue *papier maché* hill.
Children thrill in taking turns
jumping from Fishermen's Pier.
Pull back. Pousadas line the
backdrop beach, backdropped by
rolling, gentle hills. Watch gulls
fly in and out, freefall, glide.
Pull back. Our hammock smiles on
this scene, its fishnet weave
two ship sails in springtime breeze.
Pull back to two glass sliding doors,
two panes apiece: the bone-white frame
for morning's masterpiece.

<17>

TESTING THE WATERS

FORTE DEI MARMI, ITALY, 1994

pedal boat *hors d'oeuvre*
served with Mediterranean dip
mountainous meal of
marble snowcaps
looms before us
rainbow sunset our dessert

white jellyfish glide
clear sea below
we talk through courses
degrees of friendship
pedal forward
testing the waters

<18>

POEM OVERBOARD!

Birds sing, waves lap, yet
our motor drowns them out
when we hit 22 miles per.
Fresh wind blasts our hair.
Our wake provides a challenge
to the ancient Jet Skier,
so intent in his sport he's
oblivious to the fishermen,
the hunk on the shore
filling a wet suit, the
desperate men nearby
seeking telephoto lenses.
Green neon Wayfarers
reflect blue-white skies,
hide a water skier's eyes.
Sun's corona breaks through
clouds, over good friends:
pleasure cruise flanked by
green marsh grasses.
Speed suddenly picks up as
sunshine spreads its
summer promise over our
Maurice River Sunday.
Another curve comes
and I wonder if I'll be shouting
Poem overboard!
before we share sunset
over Delaware Bay.

<19>

View from "The Delta Lady"

WILDWOOD, NEW JERSEY, 1993

White pinpoints of light
pirouette side by side
elevated at edges
as the eye sees
four dancers' bodies
craft a right angle
multiplied in numbers,
designing Victorian gingerbread
in angles
and movement
and brilliance —
a zigzag in perfect symmetry
line dancing in
light summer breeze

river ripple
restaurant railing
whoever thought
one fanciful string of light
could create such
shimmering ballet?

<20>

FACETING FEELINGS

JERSEY SHORE, 1991

priceless jade eyes
kinetic-kind smile
flaxen topaz hair
brushed by balmy breezes
i'd like to take you
under amethyst sky
by sapphire sea
onto golden sand
put diamond to boardwalk
carve our initials
and wait
and watch
and see
whether wood
weathers away or
weathers the storms
see if onyx surf spares
diamond dust on sand
shining
or washes it away
traceless

<21>

Sunrise on the White Oak Chair

HOLLYCROFT BED & BREAKFAST,
SPRING LAKE, NEW JERSEY, 1997

Lay your head against
the peeled wood headpiece.
Cast your eyes left, right. Note
how the cut curved pieces
bend at just the right places.
Two could fit snugly, fill
this chair of criss-crossed logs,
sanded to supple smoothness.
True, this is not a chair
designed for comfort, but
place two lace-trimmed pillows
against the small of your back,
have tea and honey in a holly
china cup at your side, then
watch the sun lift gently,
reflect off the lake brilliantly
beyond this coastal forest.
You will have all
the comfort you need.

<22>

MIDDLEVILLE

firefly fireworks
light long
dappled grass

brief blinks of
brilliant light
counterbalance night

clear-clean brook gurgles
shimmers bluish silver
in full moonlight

two deer quietly
graze roadside
winding road

stays silent
only stars
ride the pavement

almost picture-perfect
scene fills my view,
all that's missing: You.

<23>

BLUE HERON BALLET

LAFAYETTE, NEW JERSEY, 2008

Cycling Decker Road's gentle slopes,
a large shadow flickers asphalt,
looming, turning my attention skyward.
Biking becomes brake-slamming.

Above, two great blue heron
circle Paulinskill River in aerial ballet,
pivot through sky, always eye-to-eye:
two facing cars on a Ferris wheel.

Gracefully they spin . . . five minutes, ten.
Sole witnesses to their airy reverie:
white steeple of Lafayette Federated, I,
the cloud-dashed azure Sussex sky.

<24>

MORNING

◇————————◇

A NEW JERSEY MOMENT, 1993

There is no darkness today.
In the three-quarter-inch bevel curves
between the shade and sill
seeps light.

Quietly it pulls its way
onto his dark hair
fanned across the pillow,
framing his sleeping face.

It reaches the mirror,
reflects through the eyelets
of our lace canopy,
lands in star-like display
against the white ceiling.

Sheets rise and fall
to quiet breathing
Even the dust particles
join in general stillness.

Before the alarm, shower,
shave, dress, travel routine
comes the brief moment:
happiness captured
in the distillation
of our quiet dawn.

<25>

Birdbath Bash

Upon waking, we head downstairs
into our 1930s-era kitchen:
milk-white cabinet doors
stenciled with pink hearts,
tiger-maple oak table
set for our welcome.

Above the kitchen sink,
through the two windows,
we've cobbled together
a birdbath: large copper plate
half a century old, brought
by my parents, from Turkey,

positioned on a cement block
to improve our viewing.
I'm learning a lot about
human nature online.
I'm starting to prefer
the company of birds:

notice how the robin
sips, breaks, sips,
while the solitary dove
takes longer sips, as if
partaking in high tea.
Caterpillar walks the edge.

<26>

Wrens are a visual treat.
Four of five of them
splash water within
their wings, seeming
so happy, seeming to
have the time of their lives.

I rarely had time to
notice these tiny things
when working full-time.
My hand pulls your waist
closer as we stand together,
enjoy this birdbath bash.

Your hair is turning gray now,
still frames your sleeping face
beside me, nightly, all these years.
Your constant love and calm, a balm
against a world in daily chaos,
a world, increasingly, for the birds.

<27>

FOUR
SEASONS
OF FORM

Spring Garden Sonnet/Acrostic

Lafayette, New Jersey — Poem written Winter 2013;
Memorial Garden begun Spring 2018

Safe from the city's chaos and with time now on our hands,
perhaps it's time to make past dreams reality. I know —
recall how roses framed the violets within. To grow
it all — petunias, buttercups, and more — we have the lands;
now nestled in our vivid yellow farmhouse several years,
good time to try out something new, enjoy as old age nears.

Got shovels, gloves, my red Radio Flyer wagon yet —
a remnant from my childhood, the seventies, perhaps;
remember how my father pulled the two of us some laps,
down driveway, up the street, the grass just cut
     and freshly wet,
even Mom out, gardening. *Our* past. New artistry:
nice touch to build a garden out here, in their memory.

<31>

Summer Rhyme

Little Falls, New Jersey — Summer 1985

Perhaps it was the light of dawn
that made me feel alive, refreshed
with morning dew upon the lawn,
contentment dancing in my head.

Perhaps it was the outdoor breeze,
a lilac-rose scent in the air
that made me stop and sigh with ease
and wave my fingers through my hair.

Perhaps it was the turquoise sky
the clouds meandering to the west
which put a pleasant feel inside,
gave overwrought nerves time to rest.

Perhaps it was that time of year:
winter behind and life like new
that touched my heart and killed my fear,
unleashed my smile for public view.

Perhaps it was the light of dawn,
the outdoor breeze of turquoise blue.
It could have been the time of year.
Perhaps it was my meeting you.

<32>

AUTUMNAL TRIOLET

Do you have anything to share aside
from despair? I ask quiet forest floor.
Bare bark surrounds me. (Perhaps it replied.)
Do you have anything to share aside
from heartache? Silence. A pause in my stride
is all this autumn will bring. Nothing more.
Do you have anything to share aside
from despair?! I ask quiet forest floor.

<33>

GAZELLE GHAZAL

Ice encroaches the window, shedding snakeskin on glass.
Sharp claws of the leopard pull stories onto grass.

To shed your skin again, or to rebel?
Take on the speed and grace of the gazelle.

The trees are wistful. Sky — so gray, so *blah*.
I look on snow and dream of Africa.

Somewhere a gazelle scans the same stars.
Firewood burns. A tree hit by lightning. Same scars.

Champagne pops. A gun fires. Together they fall.
Wind lifts, carries the mournful mating call.

Ice melts. Sun rises. Tomorrow turns today.
You shouldn't need shackles for shadows to stay.

<34>

BACK TO
REALITY

strike matches, hold
crucifix candelabra
protection small comfort

flickering frailty faces
shrewd slamming spirits
hammering frosted glass

ethereal coffins
release Undead in
salivating swarms

first seeming fragile
hardly harmful, but
lower defenses — open door

screams go unheard
amidst frenzied fluttering
cannibalistic charm

coldly calculating
bloodthirsty Nosferatus
begin relentless draining

sharpen that stake
string that garlic
such naïveté

some say Draculas
some say snowflakes
winter — *never* — dies

<37>

Impressions of a Winter's Snowfall

I dread the white stuff with each passing day
as my skin becomes chapped and complexion turns gray
and my eyes become teary and my nose starts to run
and my toes start to freeze and feel soaked and numb
and I look for the sun where the sun ought to be
and find heavy cloud cover and no solace to see
for it keeps coming down and I can't turn it off
and cold wind sears my lungs and I get back my cough
and my lips become chapped and a canker sore forms
and handkerchiefs pile up by the laundry room door
and my back starts to hurt from constant bending down
my face out of wind and my eyes to the ground
where I see black slush where once all was clean
and white is the color now covering green
and leaving me dampened in clothing and spirit
and nothing they do can totally clear it
so it stings at my eyes in a locust-like blight
as my hair becomes stringy and dotted in white
and matted in places, and greasy, and wet
and I wash and it's still wretched, to my regret,
and my room is a constant stream of mud and debris
and the medicine I take does no good for me
so I cough and spit mucus and barely can breathe
and my fever goes higher and I continue to seethe
that I have to wear gloves and boots and a jacket
that never is warm enough — listen, I've had it!

You can make snowmen and ski 'til you drop.

Give me some quiet and MAKE THIS ALL STOP!

<38>

EPILOGUE

WATERMELON MAN

Succulent fruit, spinning green
in gentle black water, bouncing

against fishing boats
against each other

sorting out their
places and personal spaces

this water — a way station
those carrying them

conductors to a destination
even they will not know.

<41>

ABOUT THE POET &
THIS COLLECTION

ACROSS FIVE DECADES — from the 1970s to the 2010s — David Messineo has methodically carved his place into New Jersey's often-untold poetic history. From his start as a child poet in 1971 (and later published in *The Best Student Poetry in New Jersey*, 1981 Edition), he continued with his craft, writing new poems every year since that start — and has put himself into the uncommon position of being able to honestly offer a Golden Anniversary Poetry Tour when he turns 59 years old, which is among his many forthcoming projects and personal goals.

Messineo is widely known as the Publisher and Poetry Editor of *Sensations Magazine*, for which he has received several awards: national American Literary Magazine Awards, 1994-1996; Jefferson Award for Public Service, 2009; William M. Dwyer Award for Journalism in New Jersey History, 2011. He is among the 20 longest-serving poetry editors and independent literary magazine publishers still active in America, and runs one of the 25 longest-lasting poetry reading series still active in America, the *Sensations Magazine* Creative Events Series.

Many of our more prominent U.S. literary magazine and poetry book publishers are also poets in their own right. Messineo falls within this group, as author of eight published poetry books, six of which have been out-of-print from 13 to 25 years as of 2019: *First Impressions*, *Suburban Gothic*, *A Taste of Italy*, *A Taste of Brazil*, *Restoration*, *Formal*, *The Search for the Sapphire Robe*, and *Historiopticon* (the last of which is still available online, at www.blurb.com).

<42>

ETWEEN THESE EIGHT poetry collections, and his national and international tours promoting them, David Messineo is the only New Jersey poet thus far in the 21st century to be featured in all 21 New Jersey counties; in all 50 states; and on six of the seven continents. (In January 2017, Fiction Editor Marilyn Hartl read one of his poems on the Antarctic continent, completing his goal.) Across the decades, he has become known as a poet who writes passionate, thought-provoking, well-crafted poetry about American history, social injustice, legal and political issues, and domestic and international concerns: recapturing the past, playing with time, envisioning and encouraging us toward a better future. By his own admission, the term "nature poet" likely would be among the last to come to mind when thinking of the breadth and scope of his literary output.

His ninth collection, *Twenty Minutes of Calm* — also his first collection published by The Poet's Press — changes that, and pulls together twenty of his poems on nature, scene, and season, both in form and in free verse. This collection is a blend of new and previously unpublished poetry; revisions of poems from some of his past collections; and reprints of some poems from his now-out-of-print books. To support and promote this book, Messineo will be offering a "20 Minutes of Calm" Poetry Tour from August 2019 to December 2020, in New Jersey, New York, and select other states. If you need twenty minutes of calm in your life, go see Messineo on this tour: an enduring class act in an increasingly crass 21st century America. All confirmed tour dates and locations are listed at the Events + Book Tour button at www.sensationsmag.com.

<43>

ABOUT THE POEMS

PRELUDE

The Palace of Nine Perfections
Written April 29, 1997.

The Palace of Nine Perfections is a series of twelve Chinese scrolls of ink and colored silk, painted by Yuang Jiang in 1691. According to an August 16, 2012 article by Holland Carter in *The New York Times*, *The Palace of Nine Perfections* is an interpretation of an actual place, "said to have existed near the present-day city of Xi'an, and to have covered so much ground that its many pavilions could be visited only by horseback." I selected a detail from this painting — standing at one of the pavilions — and from that vantage point envisioned this poem. *The Palace of Nine Perfections* is owned by the Metropolitan Museum of Art in New York, NY, listed as Accession Number 1982.125a-1, and may be viewed online at this link: www.metmuseum.org/toah/works-of-art/1982.125/. This is one of my rotating "core poems," read frequently in public over the past 20 years. I'm pleased to bring it back again to open my first collection of nature poems.

TWENTY MINUTES OF CALM

Moment at Lake Atsion
Written April 25, 2015.

Friends of mine have coordinated an annual gathering of poets, artists, and creatives at the rentable cabins at Lake Atsion in New Jersey. I have taken part in this occasionally. In this particular year, I was looking out the back screen of the cabin onto the lake, where pine cones were draping into the water. I was seated in one of the Adirondack-style wooden chairs on the porch, writing in the moment. This is the first publication of this poem in any form. The cover photograph of the book is taken from this location, as well.

<45>

Eagle's Reach
Written Summer 2005.

This poem, a Burns stanza (named after Scottish poet Robert Burns), was inspired by a particular set of cave paintings in Wollemi National Park, which is in New South Wales in eastern Australia. Though I did make it to Australia in 2013, I did not visit this national park, but found the paintings online. This link talks extensively about the discovery and initial exploration of the cave paintings at Eagle's Reach in 2001-2003: www.wsws. org/en/articles/2003/08/rock-a05.html. The handprint paintings that inspired this poem, a small portion of the larger discovery, may be viewed at the 8:00-8:15 minute mark in this YouTube documentary, which was filmed at Eagle's Reach: www.youtube.com/ watch?v=wQ5qVccmoOs.

Saturday Morning,
Pousada Mar de Búzios
Written October 8, 2005.

I took my first trip to Brazil between August and October 2005. Búzios is a city in Brazil about an hour north of Rio de Janeiro, and the Pousada Mar de Búzios was the name of the small bed and breakfast, which featured rooms with hammocks on balconies, facing Fisherman's Pier, and offering a water view and other pleasant scenery. From behind the glass doors leading to the balcony, I wrote this poem, where each *Pull back* refers to pulling the camera zoom lens back and re-snapping the same photo, from different angles, in poetry. Look up "Pousada Mar de Búzios" online, and book the second floor balcony room if you want to enjoy more than this poem. This is another of my rotating "core poems," read frequently in public.

Testing the Waters
Written August 10, 1994.

My first vacation to Europe came in the Summer of 1994, when I joined my family for a 21-day Tauck tour through Italy. At Forte dei Marmi, I was able to rent a pedal-boat, heading into the Mediterranean Sea. When I spun around to face the shore, my jaw dropped at the beautiful site of the Apennine Mountain range backdropping the beach. What looked like snow caps actually was peaks of white marble, a point that made it into the poem.

<46>

While this does not depict the precise spot that inspired the poem, you can get a sense of the scenery from the main image at this website: www.myforte.it/

Poem Overboard!
Written June 2, 1990.
I was one of four friends who rented a fishing boat for a one-day excursion down the Mullica River in southwestern New Jersey, and into Delaware Bay. Some photographs from this trip were featured in *Sensations Magazine* Issue 20, "Scenic New Jersey." The poem describes happenings of the day, and I nearly did lose my handwritten original when the boat suddenly and unexpectedly increased speed at one point in the trip.

View from *The Delta Lady*
Written September 11, 1993.
The Delta Lady was a tour boat docked near the entrance to Wildwood, NJ, just on the right when crossing the bridge onto the island. I was viewing the boat at night from a nearby dockside restaurant, and fixated on the one "fanciful string of light" and its interplay of light and shadow reflected on the water. In my Far East-inspired master bedroom in Lafayette, New Jersey, three lanterns are interconnected by one fanciful string of lights, creating a similar interplay of light and shadow on the white high-gloss ceiling — a personal interior design detail inspired by this poem.

Faceting Feelings
Written April 4, 1991.
This love poem was inspired by one of the many "loves that did not last" in my life, and was the best and most lasting thing that came out of that particular relationship. (As it turned out, the aftermath of that breakup led me a few months later to Fire Island in the summer of 1991, where I met the love of my life that lasted.) Still, I consider this a beautiful little poem, and its approach and imagery warranted its comeback in this collection.

<47>

Sunrise on the White Oak Chair
Written February 1, 1997.
Sensations Magazine conducted a Writers' Retreat at Hollycroft Bed & Breakfast in Lake Como, New Jersey — an Adirondack-styled cabin B&B then, which is now a private home. This poem was written about a chair made of white oak-tree branches that was a prominent fixture in the living room there.

Middleville
Written July 12, 1995.
Throughout my life, I have taken drives into towns in New Jersey, just to see if there was anything of interest. An upscale restaurant called The Middleville Inn drew me into this town, where I parked the car, and walked downhill on a quiet, clear summer night to a guardrail, and looked at the hillside directly ahead, which was ablaze with fireflies lighting on and off. That, and the other scenery I experienced that evening, inspired this poem.

Blue Heron Ballet
Written Spring 2008.
Part of the reason I moved to Sussex County, New Jersey was for quiet pleasures: seeing the stars at night while living in New Jersey, enjoying the 26 miles of bike paths a few blocks from my house, and more. I was bicycling along Decker Road in Lafayette, when I looked up and saw two blue herons flying in a circle while facing each other. For this collection, I have re-titled the poem from its more wordy original, "Ballet Over Lafayette, New Jersey."

Morning
Written May 2, 1995.
I was living in Secaucus, New Jersey, where I had a colonial-style canopy bed facing alongside the bedroom window from the third floor condo unit. This poem captured that moment: a love poem for the love of my life, written as a birthday gift. This is one of my "core poems," read frequently in my public readings, in New Jersey and around the world.

<48>

Birdbath Bash
Written October 6, 2018.

This poem offers a moment of personal time travel, is the most recent poem in this collection, and achieves its first publication of any kind here. This poem picks up where "Morning" left off, heading downstairs from the bedroom into the kitchen, and observing activity in the birdbath. While it is written 23 years after "Morning," it could be taking place a few minutes later — making the poem double as a commentary on long-term relationships, and how time sometimes can seem to stand still even after years have passed.

FOUR SEASONS OF FORM

Spring Garden Sonnet/Acrostic
Written February 21, 2013.

This is the last of a spring garden-themed series of four poems written 40 years apart, and is both a sonnet and an acrostic. For this collection, I have re-titled the poem from its original "Reconstruction of the Spring Garden." I now have a memorial garden off the side entrance of home, bringing this poetic cycle to a nature-enhancing conclusion.

Summer Rhyme
Written June 26, 1985.

One year after graduation from college, I wrote this poem, which often was my concluding poem at public readings in the 1980s. For this collection, I have re-titled the poem from its original "Perhaps it was the light of dawn." I always liked this upbeat poem, and am pleased to bring it back for a new book and tour.

Autumnal Triolet
Written October 31, 2002.

This quiet mood piece is in the standard triolet format, and gets its second moment in the spotlight here.

<49>

Gazelle Ghazal
Written January 31, 1998.

One of my artistic goals is to have all the poems I have written published in a book format that pleases me, within my lifetime. This poem never quite fit into any of my previous or planned thematic projects, but it works sufficiently to conclude this four-poem form set. This was my first attempt at writing a ghazal, and this is its first publication.

BACK TO REALITY

Some Say Draculas
Written March 2, 1994.

Who needs Alaska when you can enjoy the harsh, often relentless winters of New Jersey?

Impressions of a Winter's Snowfall
Written January 18, 1994.

This is the oldest poem in this collection, in a common basic rhyme style I turned to often in my early years of writing poetry. I have revised the last two lines in this version, to give this poem a contemporary flavor for the 2019-2020 *20 Minutes of Calm* Tour.

<50>

EPILOGUE

Watermelon Man

Written October 5, 2005.

I wrote this poem in Manaus, Brazil, remembering an earlier moment from my side trip a few days earlier, to Maués, Brazil. It was the sixth in a series of eight "Compass Point" poems, inspired by scenes in different directions from a particular point within that city. All kinds of journeys — poetic or otherwise — lead us to destinations we cannot anticipate when we start out. I anticipate that will be the case with the *20 Minutes of Calm* Tour, and feel this is a nice atmospheric piece to conclude our journey together in this collection. I wish you well with where life's journey takes you next, and thank you for reading these reminiscences of the inspiration for these poems.

<51>

CREDITS AND EDITS

◇———————————————————◇

THE AUTHOR WISHES to thank and acknowledge these presses for originally publishing the following poems, which are in original or revised editions in this collection:

The Palace of Nine Perfections. From *Formal* (Snake Hill Press, 2006).

TWENTY MINUTES OF CALM
Moment at Lake Atsion. First publication here.
Eagle's Reach. From *Formal* (Snake Hill Press, 2006). Originally titled "Eagle's Reach, Wollemi National Park, Australia."
Saturday Morning, Pousada Mar de Búzios. From *A Taste of Brazil* (Snake Hill Press, 2006).
Testing the Waters. From *A Taste of Italy* (Snake Hill Press, 1994). Originally titled "Testing the Waters: Forte dei Marmi."
Poem Overboard! Originally published in *Sensations Magazine* Issue 20, "Scenic New Jersey," 2000.
View from *The Delta Lady.* From *Suburban Gothic* (Snake Hill Press, 1999).
Faceting Feelings. From *Suburban Gothic* (Snake Hill Press, 1999).
Sunrise on the White Oak Chair. Originally published in *Poetic Reflections of Monmouth County* (Northwind Publishing, 2004).
Middleville. From *Restoration* (Snake Hill Press, 2002).

<52>

Blue Heron Ballet. First published in *Voices From Here* (Paulinskill Poetry Project LLC, 2009). Originally titled "Ballet Over Lafayette, New Jersey."

Morning. Version first published in *Meta-Land: Poets of the Palisades II* (The Poet's Press, 2016).

Birdbath Bash. First publication here.

FOUR SEASONS OF FORM

Spring Garden Sonnet/Acrostic. From *Historiopticon* (Freedom-of-the Press, 2013). Originally titled "Reconstruction of the Spring Garden."

Summer Rhyme. From *Suburban Gothic* (Snake Hill Press, 1999). Originally titled "Perhaps it was the light of dawn..."

Autumnal Triolet. From *Formal* (Snake Hill Press, 2006).

Gazelle Ghazal. First publication here.

BACK TO REALITY

Some Say Draculas. From *Restoration* (Snake Hill Press, 2002).

Impressions of a Winter's Snowfall. Revised. From *Suburban Gothic* (Snake Hill Press, 1999).

EPILOGUE

Watermelon Man. From *A Taste of Brazil* (Snake Hill Press, 2006).

<53>

The Poet's Press

PITTSBURGH, PA

So this then is *Twenty Minutes of Calm,*
designed and typeset
at The Poet's Press in Ye manner of
The Roycrofters (1895-1915) of East Aurora, New York.
The main text typeface is Bookman.
The poem titles are in P22 Arts and Crafts Hunter,
a display face based on letterforms
created at The Roycroft Shops by Dard Hunter.
Ornaments under the poems are by Dard Hunter
& other Roycroft artists.

Cast into digital form
this Third day of August, 2019
at Pittsburgh, Pennsylvania.